THE LIFE AND ART OF

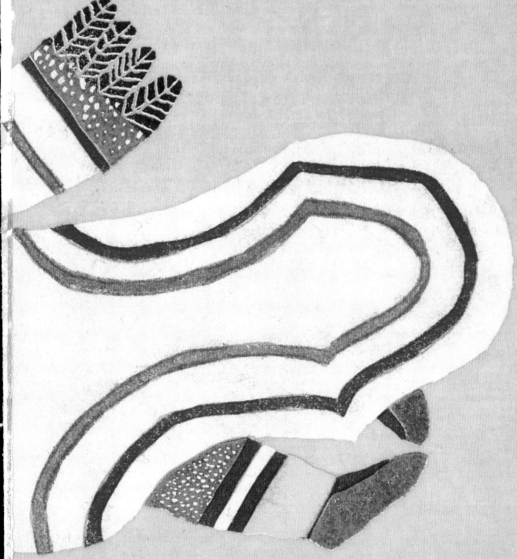

NINGIUKULU
TEEVEE

Nunavummi

The Nunavummi reading series is a Nunavut-developed levelled book series that supports literacy development while teaching readers about the people, traditions, and environment of the Canadian Arctic.

Published in Canada by Nunavummi, an imprint of Inhabit Education Books Inc. | www.inhabiteducationbooks.com

Inhabit Education Books Inc.
(Iqaluit) P.O. Box 2129, Iqaluit, Nunavut, X0A 1H0
(Toronto) 614 Mount Pleasant Road, Unit 1, Toronto, Ontario, M4S 2M8

Printed in Canada.

Library and Archives Canada Cataloguing in Publication

Title: The life and art of Ningiukulu Teevee / written by Napatsi Folger.
Names: Folger, Napatsi, 1983- author.
Series: Nunavummi reading series.
Description: Series statement: Nunavummi reading series
Identifiers: Canadiana 20230131506 | ISBN 9781774506448 (hardcover)
Subjects: LCSH: Teevee, Ningiukulu, 1963-—Juvenile literature. | LCSH: Inuit women artists—Nunavut—Biography—Juvenile literature. | LCSH: Inuit artists—Nunavut—Biography—Juvenile literature. | LCSH: Inuit art—Juvenile literature. | LCGFT: Kinngait (Nunavut)—Biography—Juvenile literature.| LCGFT: Biographies.
Classification: LCC N6549.T42 F65 2023 | DDC j709.2—dc2

ISBN: 978-1-77450-644-8

This project has been made possible in part by the Government of Canada.

THE LIFE AND ART OF NINGIUKULU TEEVEE

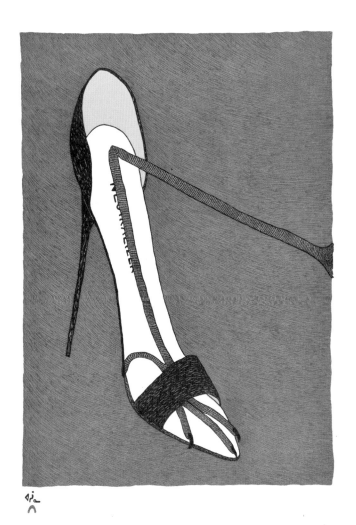

WRITTEN BY
Napatsi Folger

Who Is Ningiukulu Teevee?

Ningiukulu is an Inuk woman from Kinngait, Nunavut. Kinngait is on Baffin Island, just west of the territorial capital city, Iqaluit.

Ningiukulu is a famous artist. She has created prints and drawings that have been published in books and shown all over the world. She's also an author, wife, mother, and grandmother. She is very busy!

Ningiukulu Teevee

Bird of Spring by Abraham Etungat in front of the Vancouver Art Gallery

Early Life

Like many Inuit, Ningiukulu spent a lot of time with her grandparents growing up. Her grandfather **Abraham Etungat** was also a famous artist. He is best known for his sculptures of birds with raised wings. She used to watch him carve for hours.

Creativity runs in Ningiukulu's family! Her parents, Kanajuk and Joanasie Salamonie, were both actors. They were in the 1976 movie *Nanook Taxi*.

Ningiukulu's father also sometimes enjoyed carving and painting in watercolour. Ningiukulu remembers getting in trouble as a girl for using up all her father's art paper for drawings.

Kanajuk and
Joanasie Salamonie

Kinngait, Nunavut

Ningiukulu grew up in Kinngait during the 1960s and 1970s. She remembers the day the first TV came into town. She said it was very quiet outside. Usually there were lots of kids playing and making noise. Her friend told her that **Pitaloosie Saila** got a TV. When they walked over, all the kids in town were piled in the doorway to see it.

Falling in Love with Stories

A lot of Ningiukulu's art is inspired by Inuit stories and legends. When she was a little girl, Elder **Mialia Jaw** visited her class and told them Inuit legends. Ningiukulu said listening to the legends put pictures in her head.

This print is Ningiukulu's modern take on the story of the owl and the raven. In that story, the owl gives the raven *kamiik*. Ningiukulu imagines if the story happened in modern times and the raven was gifted high heels instead.

Neutralizer by
Ningiukulu Teevee, 2016
62 cm x 44 cm,
stonecut on paper

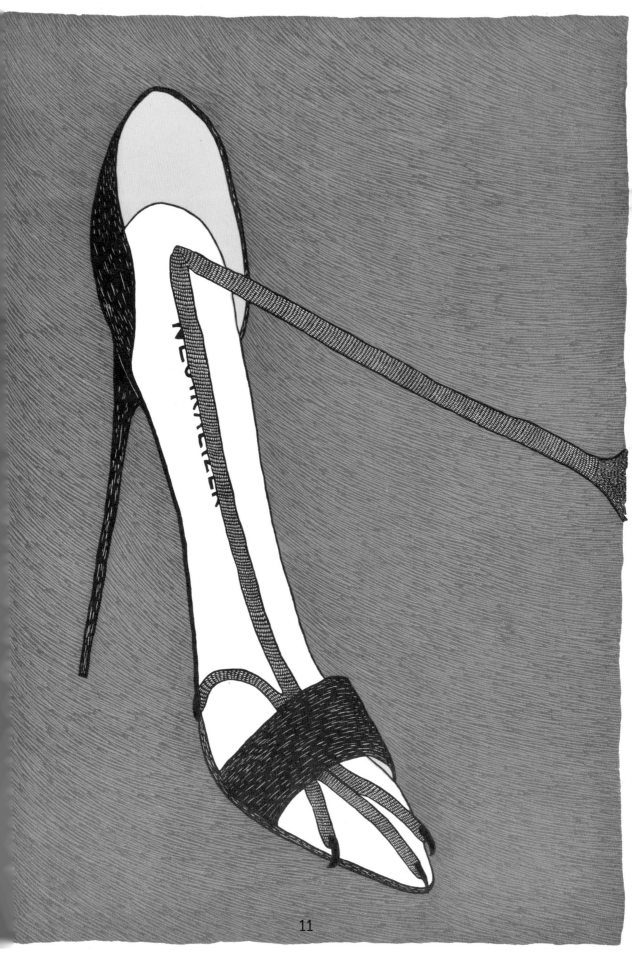

Ningiukulu is a self-taught artist. She has always watched other artists at work. She has listened to Elders tell stories and let her imagination guide her art.

She likes to work with lots of different materials, including some things you might have in your own pencil case! She has used pencil crayons, felt pens, chalk, fine liners, and acrylic and watercolour paints.

Untitled by
Ningiukulu Teevee, 2013
111.5 cm x 76 cm,
coloured pencil and ink
on paper

Ningiukulu remembers the day she first became serious about art. She heard **Jimmy Manning** on the radio asking people to come to the West Baffin Eskimo Co-operative to give art a try. She wasn't very good at first, but she worked hard. She kept practising and getting better. Now she is one of the most well-known Inuit artists today.

The West Baffin Eskimo
Co-operative in Kinngait, Nunavut

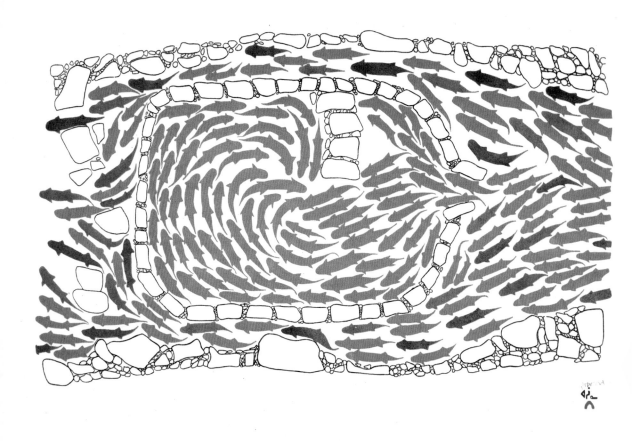

Saputiit (Handmade Fish Weir)
by Simionie Teevee, 2017
47 cm x 67 cm,
stonecut and stencil on paper

Falling in Love with Simionie

By the time Ningiukulu was a young woman, art wasn't the only thing that had caught her eye. She fondly remembers going to see local band Sikusiilaq play at the community hall in 1980. She thought the handsome guitarist and lead singer, **Simionie Teevee**, had a nice voice. They began dating, and in 1984 they got married. They have been together ever since!

Ningiukulu had three children with Simonie. Many of her drawings and prints are inspired by her life as a mother.

This picture is called *The Babysitter*. It shows a young woman riding her bike with a baby in her *amauti* and the wind blowing through her hair. Ningiukulu says she often did this with her own babies. She rode through town with them to visit family and friends.

The Babysitter by
Ningiukulu Teevee, 2020
76.2 cm x 57.8 cm,
pastel on paper

Basking Walrus by
Ningiukulu Teevee, 2019
57 cm x 72 cm,
etching and aquatint

Ningiukulu finds inspiration in all sorts of places. This etching is called *Basking Walrus*. An etching is a type of print. The walrus in this etching looks like it could be a hillside on the tundra in the summer.

The etching might be inspired by a story Ningiukulu's mother once told her. Her mother pointed to a hill near Kinngait. She told Ningiukulu about a shaman who turned himself into a walrus and climbed the cliffside. When he couldn't get back down, he settled in and became part of the landscape. He remains there today, gathering moss and flowers in the summer and snow in the winter.

Busy Woman by
Ningiukulu Teevee, 2016
76 cm x 58 cm, graphite,
pencil crayon, and ink

Ningiukulu also finds inspiration for her art in everyday life. For example, this drawing features an Inuk woman with a modern haircut, wearing jeans and a T-shirt. She is watching TV while she works with her *ulu* on a sewing project.

The Swimmer by
Ningiukulu Teevee, 2014
62 cm x 80 cm,
stonecut and stencil
on paper

Ningiukulu's variety of subjects and styles is one of the things that makes her work so popular around the world.

This print uses the shape of a fish in place of the woman's eye. It is one way Ningiukulu expresses her imaginative and fun style that makes her work so special and recognizable.

Today, Ningiukulu is still living in Kinngait. She is a proud grandmother. She likes to draw with her grandchildren at home. She encourages them and other young people to keep practising and not to get discouraged when they make mistakes. She says that one of the hardest lessons she learned was that colouring outside the lines is not the end of the world. When you make mistakes, there is always a way to make it work!

Kinngait, Nunavut

Inuit Artists

Ningiukulu is from a community of many talented Inuit artists!
Read below to learn about the other artists mentioned in this
book.

Abraham Etungat (1911–1999)
Abraham Etungat was born in 1911 in a former settlement in
Nunavut called Amadjuak. He lived on the land before moving
to Kinngait in the 1950s. He began carving when he was no
longer able to hunt due to health problems. He is best known
for his carvings of birds with raised wings. One of his most
famous works is called *Welcoming the Bird of Spring*. It is a
carving of a bird standing beside a human. It was reproduced
into large statues that became public art displays in
Vancouver, Calgary, Toronto, and Halifax.

Mialia Jaw (1934–2006)
Mialia Jaw was born in 1934 in Qimmirtuq, a camp near
Kimmirut. She spent her childhood on the land. She was
a celebrated carver, graphic artist, and storyteller. Her
husband, Joe Jaw, was also a well-known Inuk carver. They
had five children, and three of them also became artists.
Mialia was known for creating colourful artwork that shows
elements of her personal life, the natural world, and Inuit
traditional stories. Her work has been displayed in galleries
in Vancouver and Kingston, and she was part of the Cape
Dorset Annual Print Collection from 2004 to 2006.

Jimmy Manning (1951–)
Jimmy Manning was born in Kimmirut, Nunavut, in 1951. He
and his family moved to Kinngait when he was very young.
Jimmy mostly does photography, but he also does drawing,
printmaking, and carving. His grandfather is Peter Pitseolak,
who was also a photographer and an inspiration to Jimmy.
Jimmy likes to show everyday life in his community through
his photographs. Jimmy helped develop the West Baffin
Eskimo Co-operative in Kinngait. He worked there as a
manager of the printmaking studio and liked to photograph
artists at work. Jimmy's work has been featured in
collections of the Canadian Museum of History in Gatineau,
Quebec, and the Montreal Museum of Fine Arts.

Pitaloosie Saila (1942–2021)

Pitaloosie Saila was born in 1942 near Kinngait. She spent most of her childhood in hospitals in Ontario and Quebec for treatment for tuberculosis. Pitaloosie began drawing in the 1960s. She quickly became a skilled graphic artist. Her work has been featured in shows across Canada and the United States. In 1977, Canada Post made a stamp featuring her print "Fisherman's Dream." Her husband, Pauta Saila, was also a well-known sculptor. In 2004, Pitaloosie and Pauta both became members of the Royal Canadian Academy of Arts for their life's work and contributions to Canadian art.

Simionie Teevee (1959–)

Simionie Teevee is a visual artist and musician. He began drawing in 2010. He was inspired by his wife, Ningiukulu Teevee, and his father, Jamasie Teevee. He remembers watching his father draw when he was growing up. Simionie worked as an assistant lithographer at Kinngait Studios in the late 1970s and early 1980s. He is also an accomplished musician and plays many different instruments. He is in a band called Sikusiilaq Band.

Glossary of Inuktut Words

Inuktut is the word for Inuit languages spoken in Canada, including Inuktitut and Inuinnaqtun. The pronunciation guides in this book are intended to support non-Inuktut speakers in their reading of Inuktut words. These pronunciations are not exact representations of how the words are pronounced by Inuktut speakers. For more resources on how to pronounce Inuktut words, visit inhabiteducation.com/inuitnipingit.

amauti ah-MAH-oo-tee	woman's parka with a pouch for carrying a child
kamiik kah-MEEK	two skin boots
ulu OO-loo	crescent knife traditionally used by women

Nunavummi
Reading Series

The Nunavummi reading series is a Nunavut-developed levelled book series that supports literacy development while teaching readers about the people, traditions, and environment of the Canadian Arctic.

- 24–32 pages
- Sentences become complex and varied
- Varied punctuation
- Dialogue is included in fiction texts and is necessary to understand the story
- Readers rely more on the words than the images to decode the text

- 24–40 pages
- Sentences are complex and vary in length
- Lots of varied punctuation
- Dialogue is included in fiction texts and is necessary to understand the story
- Readers rely on the words to decode the text; images are present but only somewhat supportive

- 24–56 pages
- Sentences can be more complicated and are not always restricted to a structure that readers are familiar with
- Some unfamiliar themes and genres are introduced
- Readers rely on the words to decode the text; images are present but only somewhat supportive

Fountas & Pinnell Text Level: S

This book has been officially levelled using the F&P Text Level Gradient™ Leveling System.